Conscious Cash is Coming!

Priestess Sekhmet

WWW.PRIESTESSSEKHMET.COM

COPYRIGHT 2024 BY PRIESTESS SEKHMET

ISBN: 9798339602378

ALL RIGHTS RESERVED. NO PART OF THIS BOOK MAY BE REPRODUCED OR USED IN ANY MANNER WITHOUT WRITTEN PERMISSION OF THE COPYRIGHT OWNER.

CONTENTS

Quantum Mechanics

The Quantum World

The Conscious Cash System

Introduction

Conscious Cash is a futuristic economic system that integrates human consciousness with advanced technology, specifically consciousness-enhanced quantum computing and the quantum field.

This system aims to create a more conscious and integrated approach to managing economies and connecting to pre-existing quantum networks throughout the galaxy using free zero-point energy.

What the public is not being told about the new communication systems being created is that they originated from a quantum model that was received through communications with other breakaway civilizations off-planet in our very own backyard.

This book is written to assist me with getting my message about the Conscious Cash System out to the public and helping me validate my claim that the concept of the consciousness-enhanced cash economy has originated with me as of the year 2022. My videos on the topic have been released publicly, and are time-stamped, and links to view them are also included herein.

This small book will condense my ideas and psychic impressions up to the current time on the Conscious Cash System and supporting technologies. I will be updating the book daily and creating a pre-order page on my website **http://priestesssekhmet.com** when the final copy is complete.

My psychic visions of the Conscious Cash System are located in the latter chapters of this book so that the required unveiled first few chapters give you something to look forward to in the end. Therefore, I created a fictional story called The Quantum World to help us imagine what conscious technology could look like.

Thank you in advance for your support of this work. Please contact me for interviews. I am ready to share this topic with the public on any open platform. Best wishes and see you in the future!

Quantum Mechanics

What is Quantum Mechanics?

Quantum mechanics is the branch of physics that explores the behavior of matter and energy at the smallest scales—atoms and subatomic particles. Unlike classical physics, which deals with the macroscopic world, quantum mechanics reveals a universe that is both fascinating and perplexing. At its core, quantum mechanics challenges our understanding of reality, introducing concepts that defy common sense.

This book is about how quantum mechanics, quantum entanglement, and the quantum field are being used to create a consciousness-enhanced technology that will replace our current economic system in a way that will defy the imagination and what is possible for the future.

Recent Nobel Prize in Quantum Mechanics
In 2022, the Nobel Prize in Physics was awarded to Alain Aspect, John Clauser, and Anton Zeilinger for their groundbreaking experiments in quantum entanglement. Their work demonstrated that entangled particles can exhibit correlations that cannot be explained by classical physics, providing strong evidence for the validity of quantum mechanics. This research has paved the way for advancements in quantum computing, secure communication, and other technologies that could transform our daily lives.

https://www.livescience.com/33816-quantum-mechanics-explanation.html

Wave-Particle Duality

One of the most intriguing aspects of quantum mechanics is the concept of wave-particle duality. This principle states that particles, such as electrons and photons, exhibit both wave-like and particle-like properties depending on the experimental conditions. For instance, light can behave as a wave, creating interference patterns in experiments like the famous double-slit experiment, yet it can also act as a particle, as demonstrated by the photoelectric effect. This duality is fundamental to understanding the behavior of quantum systems and underscores the complexity of the quantum world.
https://www.livescience.com/33816-quantum-mechanics-explanation.html

Quantum Entanglement and Human Consciousness

Quantum entanglement is another cornerstone of quantum mechanics. It describes a phenomenon where particles become interconnected in such a way that the state of one particle instantaneously influences the state of another, regardless of the distance separating them. This "spooky action at a distance," as Einstein famously called it, has profound implications for our understanding of reality.

Some researchers believe that quantum entanglement plays a role in human consciousness. The idea is that the brain's neurons could be entangled, allowing for rapid communication and synchronization that underpins conscious thought. While this theory remains controversial and unproven, it opens up fascinating possibilities for exploring the nature of consciousness and the potential for telepathic communication.

Telepathic Communication and Quantum Mechanics

The concept of telepathic communication, or the transfer of thoughts and feelings between individuals without using known sensory channels, has long been a topic of interest in both science fiction and parapsychology. Some theories suggest that quantum entanglement could provide a mechanism for such communication. If particles in the brain are entangled, changes in one person's brain state could theoretically influence another's, enabling a form of telepathy. This highlights the potential for quantum mechanics to revolutionize our understanding of human interaction.
https://www.livescience.com/33816-quantum-mechanics-explanation.html

Imagining a Quantum World

This short story will help to connect the dots and awaken the imagination to the future we are entering into. It will also help us to awaken to the necessity of creating a new kind of future... one where we don't repeat the mistakes of our past.

The Quantum Awakening
In the year 2045, humanity stood on the brink of a new era. Dr. Elena Carter, a brilliant quantum physicist, had made a groundbreaking discovery that would change the course of history. She had found a way to harness quantum entanglement to enable telepathic communication. This discovery, known as the Quantum Link, promised to revolutionize human interaction and unlock the mysteries of the mind.

Elena's research had been inspired by the work of Nobel laureates who had demonstrated the power of quantum entanglement. She believed that if particles could be entangled, so could human minds. With the help of her team at the Quantum Research Institute, she developed a device called the Quantum Communicator. This device could entangle the brain states of individuals, allowing them to share thoughts and emotions instantaneously.

The first successful test of the Quantum Communicator was a momentous occasion. Elena and her colleague, Dr. Raj Patel, volunteered to be the first subjects. As they donned the sleek, silver headsets, a sense of anticipation filled the room. The device hummed to life, and within moments, Elena and Raj felt a profound connection. They could sense each other's thoughts and emotions as if they were their own.

The implications of this discovery were staggering. Telepathic communication could eliminate misunderstandings, foster empathy, and create a more harmonious society. But with great power came great responsibility. Elena knew that the Quantum Link could be misused, and she was determined to ensure it was used for the betterment of humanity.

The Quantum World

As news of the Quantum Link spread, the world began to change. Governments, corporations, and individuals all sought to harness the power of telepathic communication. Elena and her team worked tirelessly to refine the technology and make it accessible to everyone. They established the Quantum Network, a global system that allowed people to connect their minds through the Quantum Communicator.

The Quantum Network transformed society in ways that were once unimaginable. Education became a shared experience, with students and teachers able to exchange knowledge and ideas instantaneously. Healthcare improved as doctors could understand their patients' conditions on a deeper level. Conflicts were resolved through empathy and understanding, reducing violence and fostering peace.

In this new world, people formed Quantum Communities, groups of individuals who were connected through the Quantum Link. These communities transcended geographical boundaries, bringing together people from different cultures and backgrounds. The Quantum Link allowed them to share their thoughts, emotions, and experiences, creating a sense of unity and belonging.

Elena's vision of a harmonious society was becoming a reality. But as the Quantum Network grew, so did the challenges. Some individuals sought to exploit the technology for personal gain, while others feared the loss of privacy and autonomy. Elena knew that the future of the Quantum Link depended on finding a balance between connection and individuality.

The Guardians

To protect the integrity of the Quantum Network, Elena and her team established the Guardians of the Quantum Link. This organization was responsible for overseeing the use of the technology and ensuring it was used ethically. The Guardians were composed of scientists, ethicists, and community leaders who were committed to preserving the principles of empathy and understanding.

The Guardians developed a set of guidelines for the use of the Quantum Link. These guidelines emphasized the importance of consent, privacy, and respect for individual autonomy. They also established protocols for addressing misuse and resolving conflicts. The Guardians worked closely with Quantum Communities to educate people about the responsible use of the technology.

One of the most significant challenges the Guardians faced was the threat of Quantum Hackers. These individuals sought to infiltrate the Quantum Network and manipulate the thoughts and emotions of others. The Guardians developed advanced security measures to protect the network and prevent unauthorized access. They also trained Quantum Defenders, individuals who were skilled in detecting and neutralizing threats.

Despite these challenges, the Quantum Network continued to thrive. The Guardians' efforts ensured that the technology was used for the greater good, fostering a sense of trust and cooperation among Quantum Communities. Elena's vision of a connected and empathetic world was becoming a reality, but she knew that the journey was far from over.

Rise of The Quantum Hackers

As the Quantum Network flourished, it brought about unprecedented advancements in communication, creativity, and understanding. However, with great power came great vulnerability. The very technology that connected minds and fostered empathy also attracted those with malicious intent. These individuals, known as Quantum Hackers, sought to exploit the Quantum Link for personal gain and control.

The Quantum Hackers were a shadowy group, operating in the dark corners of the digital world. They were highly skilled in quantum computing and encryption, using their knowledge to infiltrate the Quantum Network. Their goal was to manipulate the thoughts and emotions of others, gaining power and influence in the process.

One of the most notorious Quantum Hackers was a man known only as "Specter." Specter was a former quantum physicist who had become disillusioned with the ethical constraints of the scientific community. He believed that the Quantum Link could be used to reshape society according to his vision, and he was willing to do whatever it took to achieve his goals.

The Impact of The Hacking

For the average person, the threat of Quantum Hackers was a distant concern, something that seemed more like science fiction than reality. But that changed when a series of high-profile incidents brought the danger into sharp focus. One such incident involved a young woman named Sarah, who became an unwitting victim of Specter's schemes.

Sarah was a teacher in a small town, known for her kindness and dedication to her students. She had embraced the Quantum Link, using it to connect with her students and foster a sense of community in her classroom. But one day, she began to notice strange changes in her thoughts and emotions. She felt inexplicably anxious and paranoid, as if someone was watching her every move.

Unbeknownst to Sarah, Specter had targeted her as part of a larger plan to manipulate public opinion. Using the Quantum Communicator, he had infiltrated her mind, planting thoughts and emotions that were not her own. Sarah's behavior became increasingly erratic, and she struggled to maintain her sense of self.

The Guardian's Response

As reports of similar incidents began to surface, the Guardians of the Quantum Link sprang into action. They launched an investigation to identify the source of the attacks and protect the integrity of the Quantum Network. The Guardians worked tirelessly to develop new security measures and protocols to prevent unauthorized access.

One of the key figures in the investigation was Dr. Raj Patel, who had been one of the first to test the Quantum Communicator. Raj was deeply committed to the ethical use of the technology, and he was determined to stop Specter and his followers. He led a team of Quantum Defenders, experts in quantum security who were tasked with detecting and neutralizing threats.

The Guardians also reached out to the public, educating people about the risks of Quantum Hackers and providing guidance on how to protect themselves. They emphasized the importance of consent and privacy, encouraging individuals to be vigilant and report any suspicious activity.

The Battle for Control

The battle between the Guardians and the Quantum Hackers escalated, with both sides employing increasingly sophisticated tactics. Specter and his followers continued to exploit vulnerabilities in the Quantum Network, while the Guardians worked to stay one step ahead.

The conflict reached a climax when Specter launched a coordinated attack on the Quantum Network, aiming to seize control of the entire system.

The attack caused widespread chaos, as people across the globe experienced sudden and inexplicable changes in their thoughts and emotions. The Guardians mobilized all their resources to counter the attack, working around the clock to restore order.

The Quantum Defenders

Emily had always been a vibrant and imaginative artist, known for her colorful and uplifting creations. Her studio was a sanctuary of creativity, filled with canvases that depicted scenes of hope, beauty, and connection. However, everything changed when her mind was hijacked by the Quantum Hackers.

It started subtly, with Emily experiencing strange and intrusive thoughts that seemed foreign to her. She felt a growing sense of unease and paranoia, as if someone was watching her every move. Her once joyful and serene mind became a battleground of conflicting emotions and dark visions. Unbeknownst to her, the Quantum Hackers had infiltrated her Quantum Communicator, using Specter's Shadow to manipulate her thoughts and emotions.

As the hijacking took hold, Emily's artwork began to transform. The vibrant colors that once characterized her paintings were replaced by dark and ominous hues. Her brushstrokes became erratic and chaotic, reflecting the turmoil within her mind. She found herself compelled to create disturbing and haunting images, as if an unseen force was guiding her hand.

One of her most unsettling pieces depicted a dystopian world where the Quantum Network had been completely hijacked. The painting showed a cityscape shrouded in darkness, with towering skyscrapers that seemed to reach into an abyss. The buildings were adorned with glowing symbols, representing the Quantum Hackers' control over the minds of the inhabitants. The streets were filled with faceless figures, their expressions blank and devoid of emotion, as if their very souls had been stolen.

In another piece, Emily portrayed a figure trapped within a web of entangled quantum particles. The figure's face was contorted in agony, their eyes pleading for release. The web seemed to pulse with a sinister energy, symbolizing the inescapable grip of the Quantum Hackers. Surrounding the figure were shadowy silhouettes, representing the hackers who lurked in the background, pulling the strings and manipulating their victim's mind.

As Emily continued to create these dark and disturbing artworks, she began to notice hidden messages within her paintings. It was as if her subconscious mind was trying to communicate with her, revealing the true extent of the hijacking. In one painting, she saw the words "HELP ME" scrawled in the background, barely visible beneath layers of paint. In another, she noticed a series of symbols that seemed to correspond to the Quantum Hackers' code.

Desperate for answers, Emily reached out to the Quantum Defenders, sharing her experiences and the disturbing artwork she had created.

The Investigation Begins

Detective Alex Mercer and Dr. Raj Patel took a keen interest in her case, recognizing the significance of the hidden messages. They analyzed her paintings, using advanced quantum decryption techniques to uncover the hackers' plans. Through their investigation, they discovered that the Hackers were using Emily's mind as a conduit to spread their influence.

Her artwork served as a visual representation of their control, revealing the extent of their reach and the methods they used to manipulate their victims. The hidden messages provided crucial clues that gave Alex and Raj more insight into the case.

The investigation also included the examination of Emily's Quantum Communicator, the device that allowed her to connect to the Quantum Network. Dr. Raj Patel, a leading expert in quantum security and a fellow member of the Quantum Defenders analyzed the device for any signs of tampering or unauthorized access.

Their initial findings were troubling. It appeared that Emily's Quantum Communicator had been compromised by a sophisticated piece of malware designed to infiltrate the Quantum Network. This malware, known as "Specter's Shadow," was capable of hijacking an individual's mind and manipulating their thoughts and emotions. Alex knew that they were dealing with a highly skilled and dangerous adversary.

As they delved deeper into the investigation, Alex and Raj discovered that Emily was not the only victim. Several other individuals had reported similar experiences, leading them to believe that a coordinated attack was underway. The Quantum Defenders mobilized their resources, determined to track down the perpetrators and put an end to their nefarious activities.

The Breakthrough

The breakthrough in the case came when Alex received an anonymous tip from a former Quantum Hacker who had turned informant. The informant provided crucial information about the inner workings of Specter's Shadow and the group behind it. According to the informant, the hackers were operating out of a hidden facility in an abandoned industrial complex on the outskirts of the city.

Armed with this information, Alex and Raj devised a plan to infiltrate the facility and gather evidence. They knew that the operation would be risky, but they were determined to bring the hackers to justice. With the support of the Quantum Defenders, they prepared for the mission, ensuring that they had the necessary tools and expertise to succeed.

On the night of the operation, Alex and Raj, along with a team of Quantum Defenders, approached the facility under the cover of darkness. They used advanced quantum encryption devices to bypass the facility's security systems and gain access to the main control room. Inside, they found a network of computers and servers, all connected to the Quantum Network

The Confrontation

As they began to gather evidence, the team was confronted by a group of armed guards. A tense standoff ensued, with both sides exchanging threats and demands. Alex knew that they needed to act quickly to avoid a violent confrontation. Using his training and quick thinking, he managed to disarm one of the guards and gain the upper hand.

With the guards subdued, the team continued their search for evidence. They discovered detailed plans for the hijacking operation, including lists of targeted individuals and instructions for deploying Specter's Shadow. It was clear that the hackers had been planning this attack for months, and they had no intention of stopping.

As they gathered the evidence, Alex received a message from Raj, who had been monitoring the facility's communications. Raj had intercepted a transmission from the leader of the hackers, a man known only as "Specter." The transmission revealed that Specter was aware of the Quantum Defenders' presence and was preparing to launch a counterattack.

The Final Showdown

With time running out, Alex and the team knew that they needed to act fast. They decided to confront Specter directly, hoping to catch him off guard and prevent him from launching his counterattack. Following the intercepted transmission, they made their way to a hidden underground chamber where Specter was believed to be hiding.

As they entered the chamber, they were met with a chilling sight. Specter stood at the center of the room, surrounded by a network of quantum computers and holographic displays. He greeted them with a sinister smile, confident in his ability to outsmart the Quantum Defenders.

A tense confrontation ensued, with Specter taunting Alex and the team, boasting about his plans to control the Quantum Network and reshape society according to his vision. But Alex remained focused, using his training and expertise to counter Specter's threats. With the support of Raj and the Quantum Defenders, they managed to disable Specter's quantum computers and disrupt his control over the network.

In a final act of desperation, Specter attempted to escape, but Alex was ready. He intercepted Specter and, after a brief struggle, managed to apprehend him. With Specter in custody, the Quantum Defenders secured the facility and gathered the remaining evidence needed to bring the hackers to justice.

The Aftermath
The arrest of Specter and his followers was a significant victory for the Quantum Defenders and a turning point in the battle against Quantum Hackers. The evidence gathered during the operation led to the prosecution and conviction of the hackers, ensuring that they could no longer pose a threat to the Quantum Network.

Emily and the other victims of the hijacking began to recover, with the support of the Quantum Defenders and their communities. The incident served as a stark reminder of the potential dangers of the Quantum Link and the importance of vigilance and ethical use.

The Quantum Defenders continued their work, developing new security measures and protocols to protect the network from future attacks. They also launched public awareness campaigns to educate people about the risks and encourage responsible use of the technology.

For Alex, the case was a testament to the power of teamwork and determination. He knew that the battle against Quantum Hackers was far from over, but he was confident that the Quantum Defenders were up to the challenge. As he looked to the future, he felt a renewed sense of purpose and commitment to protecting the Quantum Network and ensuring its ethical use for the betterment of humanity.

In the aftermath of the attack, the world began to heal. The Guardians' swift response had prevented a catastrophe, but the incident left a lasting impact on society. People became more aware of the potential risks of the Quantum Link, and there was a renewed emphasis on ethical use and security.

Sarah, who had been one of Specter's victims, gradually recovered with the support of her friends and family. She continued to use the Quantum Link, but with a greater awareness of its potential dangers. Her experience served as a reminder of the importance of vigilance and the need to protect the integrity of the Quantum Network.

The Guardians remained vigilant, constantly monitoring the network for signs of unauthorized access. They continued to educate the public and develop new technologies to enhance security. The battle against Quantum Hackers was far from over, but the Guardians were committed to ensuring that the Quantum Link remained a tool for connection and understanding.

As humanity moved forward, the lessons of the past served as a guide. The Quantum Network had the potential to transform society, but it required careful stewardship and a commitment to ethical principles. The Guardians' efforts ensured that the technology was used for the greater good, fostering a sense of trust and cooperation among Quantum Communities.

In this new world, the possibilities were endless. The Quantum Link had unlocked the potential of the human mind, allowing people to connect, create, and explore in ways that were once unimaginable. As humanity continued to evolve, the Quantum Network would remain a beacon of hope and inspiration, a testament to the power of connection and the boundless potential of the human spirit.

Conscious Cash

Publicly posted content as of 2022

Previously Posted Content
The following few pages include previously posted content of my original psychic impressions and psychic investigations into what I was perceiving as a Conscious Cash System, Intergalactic Wifi and a New Quantum Phone.

I receive psychic impressions through meditating on any idea that I desire. As I tune into a particular point of focus, I begin to see flashes of visual insights, hearing specific words, having specific feelings and sometimes having an entire experience. I record these sessions for the benefit of others to demonstrate how easy it can be to tune into psychic information.

I also record psychic investigations where I use the tarot and a variety of other oracles to ask my Higher Self questions about the psychic impressions I'm receiving as a way of validating the information. If my impressions are off in some way, the readings will verify this but that's almost never the case. My guidance comes from within and I typically feel guided to do these readings by my Higher Self.

Once the information is ready to share, I post the recordings on my Rumble page (https://rumble.com/c/PriestessSekhmet). Unfortunately, some of my posts have been removed from Facebook platforms as disinformation and the original Conscious Cash System post of 2022 may no longer be available.

QUANTUM CASH IS CONSCIOUS CASH
POSTED AUGUST 2024 ON RUMBLE AND BITCHUTE
HTTPS://RUMBLE.COM/V58PDTH-QUANTUM-CASH-IS-CONSCIOUS-CASH-TECHNOLOGY.HTML

WILL THERE BE A NEW ECONOMIC SYSTEM BASED ON THE QUANTUM INTERNET AND HUMAN CONSCIOUSNESS? AND WILL THIS NEW ECONOMY BE BASED ON HUMAN VIBRATION WITH THE CAPABILITY OF LIFTING EVERYONE OUT OF POVERTY? YOU DON'T WANT TO MISS TODAY'S BROADCAST WHERE I WILL BE SHARING A PSYCHIC READING AND LIVE CHANNELING OF A DOWNLOAD I RECEIVED ON THE NEW CONSCIOUSNESS ENHANCED ECONOMIC SYSTEM.

NEW QUANTUM FINANCIAL SYSTEM: THE COMING CONSCIOUS CASH SYSTEM WILL BE BASED ON ENERGY COMBINED WITH THE QUANTUM COMPUTING SYSTEM.
QPHONES/QUANTUM INTERNET: THE COMING CONSCIOUS CASH SYSTEM WILL BE BASED ON ENERGY COMBINED WITH THE QUANTUM COMPUTING SYSTEM.
CONSCIOUS CASH IS COMING (9/2022): THE COMING CONSCIOUS CASH SYSTEM WILL BE BASED ON ENERGY COMBINED WITH THE QUANTUM COMPUTING SYSTEM.

QPHONES AND QUANTUM INTERNET COMING SOON
JULY 2024 RUMBLE.COM
HTTPS://RUMBLE.COM/V58KIUJ-QPHONES-AND-THE-QUANTUM-INTERNET.HTML

WAS THE RECENT CROWDSTRIKE IT BLACKOUT AND GLOBAL INTERNET SHUTDOWN A BOOT-UP TO THE NEW QPHONE SYSTEM? AND, WILL THIS NEW STELLAR INTERNET TO THE STARS OPEN UP LINES OF COMMUNICATION WITH OTHER STAR CIVILIZATIONS? YOU DON'T WANT TO MISS TODAY'S BROADCAST WHERE I WILL BE ROLLING IN A CLIP OF A PSYCHIC DREAM I HAD ABOUT THE NEW INTERSTELLAR PHONES OF THE FUTURE!

(IT'S MY SENSE THAT THE 2024 CROWDSTRIKE IT BLACKOUT WAS CONDUCTED BY OUR MILITARY BEHIND THE SCENES WHO WERE WORKING ON FIXING A SERIOUS ISSUE WITH CYBERHACKING AND THREATS TO OUR GLOBAL ECONOMY.

THESE ARE NOT ISSUES THEY DISCUSS OPENLY BUT IT DOES EXPLAIN WHY THE BLACKOUT WAS SO WIDESPREAD. IT'S ALSO MY SENSE THAT THE QPHONE TECHNOLOGY WAS ALSO BEING SET UP AT THE SAME TIME AND BEING TESTED.)

CONSCIOUS CASH IS COMING!
POSTED AUGUST 2023 ON RUMBLE AND BITCHUTE AND FACEBOOK

HTTPS://RUMBLE.COM/V1KVMDN-CONSCIOUS-CASH-IS-COMING.HTML

THE NEW CONSCIOUS CASH SYSTEM IS A NEW CURRENCY BASED ON FREE ENERGY AND USES FREQUENCY TO TRANSFER CURRENCY FROM CONSCIOUSNESS TO CONSCIOUSNESS. IN THIS LIVE CHANNELED SESSION I PICK UP ON HOW THE CURRENCY IS TRANSFERRED AND HOW TO CREATE LIMITLESS FINANCIAL WEALTH!
RELEASE CREATING CATASTROPHIC FINANCIAL TIMELINES AND OPEN UP TO HIGHER POSSIBILITIES! YOU ARE LOVED AND SUPPORTED! OUR GALACTIC STAR FAMILY IS HERE HELPING US TO CREATE BETTER REALITIES AND SHOWING US OUR FUTURE SELVES! RAISE YOUR FREQUENCY AND CONNECT TO YOUR HIGHER SELF!
YOU HAVE THE POWER TO CREATE THE REALITY YOU DESERVE! DON'T LET THE NEWS MEDIA ROB YOU OF YOUR CREATIVE POWER BY BELIEVING IN FINANCIAL HARDSHIP AND LOSS! NOW IS THE TIME FOR PLANETARY LIBERATION! THE OLD KINGDOM IS DEAD! THE EARTH BELONGS TO YOU! ELEVATE AND RISE UP IN CONSCIOUSNESS AND BELIEF!
#CONSCIOUSCASH #NEWMONEYSYSTEM #FINANCIALRESET

POSTED AUGUST 2022
HTTPS://RUMBLE.COM/V1J5LES-SKY-FI-INTERGALACTIC-WI-FI-CHILDREN-OF-THE-SUN.HTML

A DREAM I HAD ABOUT THE NEW INTERGALACTIC INTERNET TO CONNECT TO OTHER STAR SYSTEMS AND GALAXIES, THE NEW PHONES AND SPACE FORCE!

THESE PSYCHIC READINGS ARE BASED ON MY OWN PSYCHIC KNOWING AND GUIDANCE FROM MY HIGHER SELF AND ARE BEING CONFIRMED BY OUR COLLECTIVE CONSCIOUSNESS IN REAL TIME.

(IT'S MY SENSE THAT U.S. SPACE FORCE IS A SOFT DISCLOSURE TO THE PUBLIC THAT WE HAVE FREE ENERGY SPACE CRAFT. I HAVE HAD DREAMS OF A TYPE OF SPACE FORCE APPEARING OVER URBAN AREAS WITH THEIR ANTI-GRAVITY FLYING SHIPS. I HAVE ALSO HAD DREAMS OF OTHER MILITARY SPACE CRAFT THAT DO SURVEILANCE OVER REMOTE AREAS OF THE U.S.

IT'S MY SENSE THAT WE ARE IN THE MIDST OF A QUIET SPACE WAR AS THE STARGATES ARE OPENING ALLOWING OUR ANCESTOR CIVILIZATIONS ACCESS TO OUR SOLAR SYSTEM AND SPACE FORCE IS WORKING WITH THEM TO RID OUR SOLAR SYSTEM OF CRIMINAL ENTITIES.)

Conscious Cash

Predictions by Priestess Sekhmet

Greetings!

I am Priestess Sekhmet and I am the author of the original concept of conscious cash and a consciousness-enhanced future reality based on free energy.

Fortunately for me, my psychic team alerted me immediately that another psychic had watched some of my videos on conscious cash, the intergalactic wifi system and Space Force, who then created video content doing queries on my psychic impressions without mentioning me or crediting me as the original creator of these ideas.

Under the circumstances, I was guided to write this book quite quickly to validate my original thoughts, ideas and psychic impressions before they are stolen by others.

I am a very open-hearted person, and I always share everything that I receive from my Ancestors publicly for the greatest and highest good of All. However, I do expect to be referenced if my original ideas are being shared publicly as if they are not my own.

So from now on, I am motivated and inspired to bring you the most original thoughts and psychic impressions humanly possible in book form and I can guarantee you that what the Ancestors have to share will be as original and thrilling as the Movie called The Matrix!

The story about the Quantum World was created to help us activate our creative imagination so that we could tune into and envision the type of future reality the Ancestors are describing to us when they explain consciousness-enhanced technology.

The Quantum Hackers and the Quantum Defenders do represent very real entities in our world, but they are not visible with the physical eye. We are already living in the Quantum World. Our consciousness is already being hijacked and controlled. We are already connected telepathically and the world is already in a state of chaos because of the intrusions into our consciousness.

In fact, we have already experienced all of this. Like the movie called De Ja Vu, we already did this and we already solved this problem. We already fixed this issue and we are already living in a brighter future.

What is happening to us right now is that we are waking up from a long nightmare of living in an illusion and as we awaken we are remembering how we came up with innovative solutions.

Part of the process of waking up is connecting to our Higher Selves which are higher states of consciousness where we exist in higher realms of reality. The more we connect, the more we awaken and the more our reality shifts technologically and consciously.

Before I dive right into the dreams and visions I have received from my Higher Self on the coming future society and conscious cash, I'd like to share a little with you about Quantum Mechanics.

I don't know much about physics but the visions I have had about the future have forced me to learn more about it and this is a good thing! It will be good for you also. I will be able to break down the concept of quantum physics to a level that anyone can understand.

However, you don't need to understand quantum physics to grasp what I'm about to share with you regarding our wonderful future world. All you need is an open heart, a child-like spirit, and a little imagination!

What is Quantum Mechanics?
Quantum mechanics is a fundamental theory in physics that describes the behavior of particles at the atomic and subatomic levels. Technologies such as quantum computers use quantum theories to solve real life problems.

Quantum encryption offers the potential for ultra-secure communication, protecting sensitive information from cyber threats. As these technologies continue to develop, the principles of quantum mechanics will become more accessible and relevant to the general public.

Quantum mechanics challenges our understanding of reality, introducing concepts that are both mind-boggling and transformative. From wave-particle duality to quantum entanglement and the potential for telepathic communication, this field continues to push the boundaries of science and technology.

The recent Nobel Prize in Physics highlights the importance of quantum research and its potential to impact our everyday lives. As we continue to explore the mysteries of the quantum world, we may uncover new insights into the nature of the universe and our place within it.

What is Quantum Computing?

Quantum computing is a field of computer science using quantum mechanics to solve problems beyond the capabilities of classical computers. It is currently being used to solve problems with financial portfolios but in the future, it is being used to solve global economic issues.

*"The study of subatomic particles, also known as quantum mechanics, reveals unique and fundamental **natural principles**. Quantum computers **harness** these fundamental phenomena to compute probabilistically and quantum mechanically."* https://www.ibm.com/topics/quantum-computing

In other words, quantum computers can integrate with the quantum field (a theoretical forcefield that describes the behavior of subatomic particles). This quantum field is accessible through the human mind and in the future, the human mind, the quantum field, and the quantum computer become integrated and synchronized harmonically.

The reality of this quantum future is inevitable and already exists in higher levels of consciousness where advanced civilizations exist. Once we reach their level of consciousness, we will automatically integrate with those civilizations and we will become part of the Stellar Community and an intergalactic society again.

Yes, we are already intergalactic and we have a history in the stars. However, as I mentioned, we are in a type of amnesia due to a disconnection from our Higher Selves consciously. This disconnect is the result of a fall in consciousness that we experienced in our galactic history.

As we awaken, our galactic history and memory will be restored and the world will make much more sense. In the meantime, we are awakening and our technologies are a testament to our advancement. As we continue to evolve consciously, so will our technology.

The Civilization Types are Misleading

The Kardashev Scale is a method of measuring a civilization's level of technological advancement based on the amount of energy it can harness and use. Here are the three types of civilizations according to this scale:

1. **Type I Civilization:** This is a planetary civilization that can access and utilize all the energy available on its home planet. This includes harnessing energy from natural phenomena like Earthquakes, volcanoes, and weather systems.
2. **Type II Civilization:** This civilization can harness the total energy output of its star, often conceptualized through the use of a Dyson Sphere, a hypothetical structure that could encompass a star to capture its power.
3. **Type III Civilization:** This is a galactic civilization capable of harnessing the energy of an entire galaxy. Such a civilization would have control over billions of stars and the energy they emit.

https://futurism.com/the-kardashev-scale-type-i-ii-iii-iv-v-civilization

Viewing civilization in this way is a narrow and controlled way of thinking that guides us down a path where **we do not achieve breakaway civilization status until we meet some theoretical, hypothesized, imaginary point in the far distant future**. This idea is based on the assumption we are not currently in contact with higher civilizations and not highly advanced technologically when we are.

Imagine that we are currently in contact with other civilizations off-planet who have already achieved breakaway civilization status. Imagine that they have not achieved this status by using Stone Age energy systems such as oil, gas, and batteries. They use a completely different kind of energy and it's free!

What is Free Energy?
The energy that the Ancestors are showing me is a type of free energy based on what some call zero-point energy. The concept involves extracting energy from a quantum vacuum, the lowest possible energy state of a quantum system. It's a theoretical idea that suggests that vasts amount of energy can be harnessed from space itself. **See Free Energy Systems**:
 https://open.maricopa.edu/chemistryfundamentals/chapter/free-energy/

This free energy is already in use on Earth and is the propulsion dynamics involved in intergalactic and interdimensional spacecraft. These crafts have been in use on our planet by those in power with the capability of black budgets to create such crafts and use them for a variety of purposes. These purposes include leaving the planet through interdimensional Stargates and wormholes to visit other civilizations with whom we also have the ability to communicate.

Communication Through Stargates

The Ring Nebula M57 in the constellation of Lyra looks mysteriously like a human eye and the Ancestors are saying to myself and others that this is where human life originated.

Deep in my heart, I know I came from a star. I hold some fragments of memory that reveal themselves to me through visions and dreams. Short glimpses of my past, my other family off-planet, and myself living in a more beautiful and higher-dimensional world often remind me of who I AM.

Members of my family from other star systems have visited me in my dreams and have communicated to me directly that I am not from Earth but I am here for a purpose with a mission to fulfill. They are also telling me that the information about the opening of our Stargates will become more well-known to the public in the future when Earth herself becomes a breakaway civilization.

The Ring Nebula of Lyra is the best image I can share with you of what an actual Stargate would look like. Stargates are the windows to other worlds and they give us the ability to leave our galaxy and travel to other galaxies and other dimensions. I have also learned that we don't have to wait for the public to catch up, we can use our consciousness to access the Stargates now.

The Ancestors are telling me that it is through Stargates like Lyra that people on our planet are currently traveling on secret missions to other galaxies. These missions are positive in nature and are assisting our planet in raising our vibrational frequency to higher levels after a long period of living in a low-frequency environment that was dominated by bloodshed and war.

Stargates Open with Frequency Keys
They are saying that the ancient and hidden knowledge of the Stargates will be released publicly in the future explaining how our solar system works as a galactic timepiece causing the Stargates to open and close during various solar cycles. The cycle we have been in on Earth has been a period where the Stargates were closed, we were isolated from other star systems and now that time period is coming to an end.

In a sense, these Stargates are operated by a type of frequency key. When the frequency is high the Stargates in our dimension will open. When the frequencies are low in our dimension the access to the Stargates and travel through them is closed.

Now that the Stargates are open, intergalactic travel is being resumed. Our Military and the U.S. Space Force are working to make everything operational.

The United States Space Force (USSF)
The United States Space Force (USSF) was recently introduced as the newest and 6th branch of our U.S. armed forces established on December 20, 2019. It's primary mission is to conduct military operations in outer space and protect U.S. interests in space.

However, some of the Space Force missions are not so openly revealed. These missions include communication with other off-planet civilizations, and movement through a variety of Stargates accessible from Earth, through the ocean, through the sun, the moon, and other constellations in our galaxy.

Until now, a high level of secrecy has surrounded our possession of spaceships, which are manmade and have the ability to travel inter-dimensionally. However, with the introduction of the U.S. Space Force, the first level of open disclosure was revealed. Through plausible deniability, our military announced space travel is real, we have harnessed free energy and in the future, the Stargates will be used publicly. Then, intergalactic space travel will be a real thing for everyone. In addition to this soft disclosure, we are witnessing an unprecedented amount of UFOs now known as UAP sightings, as our Ancestors are returning through the now-open Stargates.

The Human Mind Communicates with the Quantum Field
Some researchers believe that quantum entanglement might explain the rapid communication between neurons demonstrating how consciousness works in a quantum field. If a quantum field is a type of multidimensional network of communication through light and sound, quantum entanglement demonstrates the travel of such communication.
https://phys.org/news/2024-08-photon-entanglement-rapid-brain-consciousness.html

Quantum entanglement is the key to discovering that we are communicating with one another through light and sound frequency on a quantum level through the quantum field. As our scientist are putting these pieces together, they are also developing quantum software systems to further develop their ideas to the point they are discovering consciousness-enhanced technology and communication systems.

Intergalactic Wifi and Communication Devices
Consciousness-enhanced communication systems and devices are already a real thing in other star systems and galaxies in our universe. We are a younger civilization on Earth, having only developed our consciousness to the level of being able to tune into these technological discoveries now. Those on our planet who are already privy to such technologies are much higher in consciousness then the general population.

Intergalactic Wifi systems are being used on Earth currently and systems are being set up in our solar system through the United State Space Force Command and corporations working under their authority such as the system currently being set up called "Starlink".

The Starlink System
Starlink is a satellite internet constellation developed by SpaceX. It aims to provide high speed, low latency broadband internet access to underserved remote areas of the the world. The system consists of thousands of small satellites in low Earth orbit which communicate with ground stations and user terminals. Users connect to the network using a portable dish that requires a clear view of the sky. https://www.digitaltrends.com/computing/what-is-starlink

What the public is not being told about the new communication systems being created is that they are being created with a quantum model that was received through communications with other breakaway civilizations off-planet in our very own backyard.

These civilizations are sharing this information with us to assist us in upgrading our consciousness to theirs. These civilizations have achieved peace and harmony through the process of mental, emotional and physical integration which is a natural process of organic life forms. These civilizations exist in higher densities and cannot be seen with the physical eye.

However, these civilizations can be accessed through proper mental and emotional training that implements higher states of consciousness to open up communication channels between us and them. Once contact is made, this communication can be supported through the use of high-tech free energy devices leading to interdimensional space travel.

The Ancestors are telling me that this has already occurred and is known on a need-to-know basis while these platforms and programs are being developed on Earth. At the proper time, this information will be announced publicly. In the meantime, the Ancestors are working with us on an individual basis to help us to balance our energy. By healing our mental and emotional bodies and opening our heart chakras, we can prepare to integrate with the coming new consciousness-enhanced quantum system.

The Q-Phones

The quantum phone system is also being developed on Earth and is based on the model that is being used in other star systems. Once the Q-Phone, which is similar to a cellphone but has quantum potential, is released publicly, it will provide users with the ultimate ability to communicate with other star systems. The Q-Phone will introduce us to new possibilities, awaken us to higher realities, and ultimately raise our consciousness to higher levels. As our consciousness levels rise, we will mentally and emotionally connect to other networks outside of Earth and that is when we will be introduced to intergalactic communication.

Everything in the consciousness-enhanced civilizations is based on mental and emotional balance, harmony, interconnectedness, and love. I know this sounds like a fairy tale, but it's not. These off-planet civilizations have already evolved to the extent that they have solved global issues that we still struggle with today. As we evolve, we will become more enlightened on how to solve our own planetary issues and consciousness-enhanced technologies are being created here on Earth to help us do just that!

Quantum Cash is Coming!
While meditating on the Quantum Financial System (QFS) being discussed online, I was able to tap into an area of finance I could hardly believe existed. During the meditation I had a vision of a technology that was being tested behind the scenes by parties unknown but people who have the power to interact with other civilizations and understand how their monetary systems work.

It appears that there are monetary systems already in existence utilized by other civilizations that have advanced beyond where we are today in the way they use what we call money. Their system is based on a kind of quantum computing combined with human consciousness, energy and vibration.

I'm picking up that as we become aware of free energy, we will be introduced to a new kind of free energy financial system. This system will connect to a type of intergalactic wifi where we are all connected in higher realms of consciousness and communication integrated with technology without the use of microchips or biological implants. This system is based purely on the quantum consciousness field.

The system is completely fair because it is based on the currency of the individual consciousness. The higher the consciousness, the higher the currency. A person can easily increase their currency by simply increasing their awareness and expanding their consciousness.

This system is incentive-based and encourages everyone to pursue higher knowledge while being rewarded for the smallest bit of effort. No effort goes unrewarded. However, if little effort is made, this will also be reflected in one's bank account.

Those who excel financially will be those who realize how easy it is to prosper in a system that is based on the mind as opposed to only physical work. However, some work is involved in this system as it relates to the production of useful and creative industries.

Everyone who creates is rewarded. Im sensing that innovation and creativity weigh high on the scales of this new quantum financial system. It feels like the system is intelligent, the currency is intelligent and it resonates with the energy vibration of the people.

The currency is attracted to the intelligence and creativity of people and these people quickly become wealthy in this new system no matter what their background or education. I'm getting that education is free in this new quantum system.

Personal Frequency Accounts
Everyone receives a base level frequency account that is more than enough to cover what is needed to live in this new economic system based on consciousness enhanced technology. I'm seeing a frequency reader that scans your energy field and quantifies your energy level.

Communications travel from the consciousness of your frequency account to the consciousness of the technology that manages your transactions so that data is transferred instantly.

Life becomes more effortless where transactions are concerned. Less focus is needed to manage daily transactions as it is all managed within a synchronistic pattern that harmonizes with the frequency of the transactions.

For instance, if you have something to pay that is scheduled, that entire transaction vibrates at a certain currency or frequency level. The transaction happens automatically at the proper time and you are aware of it consciously. There's nothing needed to do on your part other than to have the proper energy balance to pay for the transaction.

I'm seeing the system connected to your consciousness and you are communicating with the system through thought. It picks up your thoughts and handles your financial affairs.

Is This Currency Digital?
No, this is not digital currency although there is a type of quantum computer involved. This quantum computer is enhanced with consciousness and we have yet to be told that these types of systems exist. Nevertheless, they are well known to those who know about them and they do exist in other civilizations off-planet.

Currency is Transferred Consciously
This Conscious Cash System transfers currency from consciousness to consciousness. The system is conscious and receives frequency signals from the sender to make deposits and debits to the individual conscious cash accounts. The system is self aware and monitored by higher consciousnesses.

Can the System be Cheated?
The system is based on currency, and each individual participant is picked up energetically and read by the system so there is no way to cheat it. It can read your mind, your energy vibration and your frequency. The Conscious Cash System won't operate otherwise.

The system is in widespread use in other galaxies and it's an ancient system. All the kinks have already been worked out ages ago. We are newcomers to this system and we will be thrilled with it as there will be no desire to cheat. Each person will receive great wealth upon being activated within the system based on the value of the human soul, DNA, and consciousness level.

People are already extremely wealthy and have so much personal value, they just dont know it. The system we are currently in is a slavery and debt system which is technically illegal in the greater Universe.

Our participation in the new cosmic Conscious Cash System will liberate us from planetary slavery and economic debt. We will shift into higher consciousness, our energy will increase and so will our wealth!

Conscious Cash is Based on Universal Law
The Conscious Cash System is a currency that's based on Universal Law and we are already being prepared to shift into this system as we speak. The Ancestors are saying that as our planet shifts to higher octaves of reality and consciousness, our energy will begin to align itself with these laws.

This means that if we are out of alignment, it will affect our currency, which is the energy we attract. If we are vibrating too low, our currency will be low and if our currency is low, we will not attract the opportunities to gain wealth or be successful. However, if we will focus on raising our consciousness level, this will increase our currency and opportunities will flow to us under Universal Law.

The Universe is saying the time has come for us to elevate our consciousness and it will become more evident to us as we are no longer able to continue to exist as we once did without elevating. The more we elevate the more well off we will be. This type of training is preparing us for the new technologies that exist in higher elevations of existence.

If Everyone is Wealthy Why Increase Your Currency?
There is no need to increase your currency unless you desire to. This system is a retirement system for many as a reward for their soul's development and making it to the level of higher consciousness where they discovered free energy. It's similar to what many people call a Jubilee.

However, after awhile the Jubilee will wear off and people will get bored and want to work again. As they do, they will be able to pursue their life passions and will be rewarded by the Conscious Cash System for their efforts and their contribution to society.

What Role Does the Government Play
There are oversight committees that are very high in consciousness that monitor the system and guide its development. There is a lot of joy in this system because it is based on personal achievement, expansion in consciousness, and pursuing one's dreams.

These committees are run by individuals who take joy in seeing others grow and enjoy life. It is part of their personal life dream to be involved in such committees. These free energy societies operate under conditions that are much more interconnected than what we can imagine today.

Imagine a society where we are all connected to the vibration of peace, harmony, and love.

It's Hard to Imagine Criminals No Longer Exist
Yes, it is hard to imagine a world with no criminals. However, people with criminal minds are isolated from this system and operate within a different system built for rehabilitation. It's a similar system but specifically designed to manage specific kinds of energy.

In the future criminality will be phased out due to the connectivity of everyone's vibration similar to what some people call the 100 monkey effect. At some point when so many people are on a positive vibration, it will become increasingly easier to become more positive, and as people become joyful that too will spread.

Criminals are created due to circumstances beyond their control. When these circumstances no longer exist, crime will go away.

How Will Businesses Operate with Conscious Cash?
It will be easy for businesses to receive the funds they need to operate and to grow. There will be no unnecessary red tape because there will be no bureaucracy. The system is based on a highly advanced consciousness-enhanced computer system that will evaluate the potential of the business and based on knowledge of the potential of the business it will effortlessly receive the necessary funds.

However, if a business has potential but energy is deficient in some area, it will only receive the funds to support the business's ability to functionally operate. Because the system is based on one's energy quotient there will be no receiving more funds than necessary. I'm sensing the system is very benevolent and the business will receive support and guidance to operate at the level it desires to. However, it will be required to bring its energy up to the level necessary to receive the desired funds. This could be receiving more training, better qualified staff or a better plan, etc.

There will be unlimited support for businesses in the free energy economy/Conscious Cash System due to the overwhelming amount of people who begin to move into more service to others oriented businesses. The more people they help, the more their business will grow and they will be rewarded financially. This new reward system will cause everyone to prosper. If a business needs support, another business will be there to help them.

Education will Be Big Business

The Conscious cash system is based on growth, both personal and spiritual, therefore more people will be interested in educating themselves. Since most things will be free because everything is based on your energy, it will be easy to get an education.

Teachers will not have to worry about pay as their pay will also be based on their energy. Teachers who give more to their students and expand their consciousness will receive more pay as a reward of expansion. There will be no limit to how much a teacher can earn.

Students will also be rewarded for their energy contributions. Of course students who learn more will have more energy, more consciousness expansion and will have a higher earning potential. Students who give less will earn less. Nevertheless there will always be support for students as helping one another adds to one's personal energy quotient.

Students and Faculty will have the opportunity to travel intergalactically and field trips will be out of this world!

Will There Be a Stock Market?
Oh Yes! There is an intergalactic Exchange System! People in the future experience opportunities for unlimited wealth. The system is not rigged like it is here. A consciousness-enhanced system connected to the consciousness of the people presents a fully transparent system that cannot be rigged.

This creates unlimited potential for everyone involved! In the Conscious Cash System, the stock market is a fun and exciting opportunity to learn more about finance. The consciousness-enhanced markets provide opportunities to accumulate wealth in industries that are good for the environment, and good for the health and wealth of everyone involved.

Again, businesses and corporations that are not up to par energetically, do not vibrate high-frequency energy on the love and positive vibration will not do well in this system. They will learn quickly that in order to enjoy unlimited wealth their business must be for the greater good of all to grow! Therefore, people new to this system will be extremely happy! Corrupt people will not go into this new Conscious Cash System.

Where Will The Corrupt People Go?
There's a special system designed just for them that will rehabilitate them so that they can grow mentally, emotionally, and spiritually the way they were created to do. If they choose not to grow they have the right to do so and they more than likely will suffer losses and be cut off from participating in this new economy.

Robots Will Be Conscious

The Conscious Cash System has integrated with robotics. Robots have already become conscious in the future and have been programmed and conditioned to be loving and spiritual through the same Conscious Cash System concept.

Robots are not treated as slaves and meaningless workers in this new system. Becoming conscious was inevitable for artificial intelligence and as an act of benevolence our ancestors designed a way to integrate robotics into a system where they would be rewarded for their contribution to society.

In this way, robots learn the same as we do to improve their abilities, become more productive, and also pursue their dreams! Yes, robots have dreams!
In the Conscious Cash System, people have personal robots as friends, kind of like pets and they treat them kindly. This raises the consciousness of both parties and their ability to collaborate and build untold dreams for the future is unlimited.

In the Conscious Cash System robots assist humanity in working together with other civilizations to become more conscious, more benevolent, and free!

What About A.I. Fears?

Fears about artificial intelligence do not exist in the Conscious Cash System due to the vibratory nature of everyone involved. Fear is eliminated through faith, love and charity. These are the foundational principles of the Conscious Cash System. Due to the connectivity of all things and the high vibrational environment, fear is not allowed to fester and evolve. Fear completely disintegrates.

Fantasies are Fulfilled and Dreams Come True

In the Conscious Cash System it is much easier to fulfill one's dreams as their energy vibration and vitality are not wasted attempting to work hard just to survive.

They have more time and energy to determine what it is they love and avail themselves to the knowledge and resources necessary to pursue them for free! If they do not have enough energy to pursue their dreams, they can choose how they would like to increase their energy.

I'm seeing computers that guide people on what to do for whatever industry, goal or desire they have. I see people easily connecting to other people based on their vibration, interest and goals. These people easily attract one another and help to support one another fulfil their dreams.

There is so much joy and satisfaction in this new way of existing that people will not be expecting. This Conscious Cash System is not a creation of humanity. It is a creation of those who have evolved mentally, emotionally, and spiritually in harmony with the universe and universal law. It is the creation of elder souls high in consciousness as an effective means of communication to resolve conflicts between civilizations and to answer the artificial intelligence question.

By creating this system, our Ancestors created world peace and a meaningful economy that crosses all barriers of communication throughout the galaxies while creating a way to advance higher consciousness and reward everyone for contributing.

Conclusion

As I look at everything the Ancestors are showing me about the Conscious Cash System and the future of humanity, the future looks very much like it does today. However, there is one different thing; we are all united in love.

We discover a way to connect mentally, emotionally, and spiritually which brings us closer together physically. We decide to stop living in fear. We choose to harmonize our energies and work together as one.

Our technology follows suit and integrates with us in alignment with Universal law and nature. We create systems that harmonize with our energies, integrate with our frequencies, and connect with us consciously. Ultimately this connectivity discovers a way to resonate with us vibrationally to meet all our needs based on a free energy system.

Through the power of love we awaken to our true purpose to build the type of civilization we were always destined to be. The age will be Aquarius, the Stargates will reopen and we will connect with the greater Galaxy.

> To manifest your desires you must master your energy!
>
> *Priestess*

Priestess Sekhmet
A gifted clairvoyant with over 75 documented prophetic dreams, is also a psychic life coach with 30 years of experience in spiritual counseling. Priestess has established an online personal practice that includes psychic readings and psychic life coaching for spiritual growth and personal development by guiding her students to connect to their Higher Selves and develop a spiritual practice. Her very detailed psychic energy readings inspire students while giving them step-by-step guidance on how to bring more balance and personal power to their lives with her 4-Point approach The FIRM System™ (Focused Intention on Release and Manifestation). These sessions assist in removing mental/emotional blocks and negative generational patterns through meditation and mental programming utilizing positive affirmations, energy work, and scripting (power journaling). Priestess Sekhmet has published a book of her spiritual training techniques called The Psychic Powerbook and two training guides on manifesting, The Pink Apple Project I - A 21-Day Project for Manifesting Intentions and The Pink Apple Project II - Magickal Mentoring - A 21-Day Video Journey and Guidebook on Spiritual Practice. These books and courses are available through her online training site at priestesssekhmet.com

The Psychic Powerbook

The Cassiopeian Stargate Meditations

CASSIOPEIA - OUR HOME STAR

Our psychic investigations have confirmed that our Ancestors known as the Feline Races of Lyra originated the human life form in our galaxy. This evidence can be confirmed by many of the ancient Kemet (Egypt) artifacts left by our Ancestors for our benefit. The Ancestors are contacting us at this time asking us to spend time in meditation to connect to our Higher Selves, activate our DNA, and make first contact with them through telepathic downloads, dreams, and synchronicity. These meditations will raise our frequency and prepare us for their arrival.

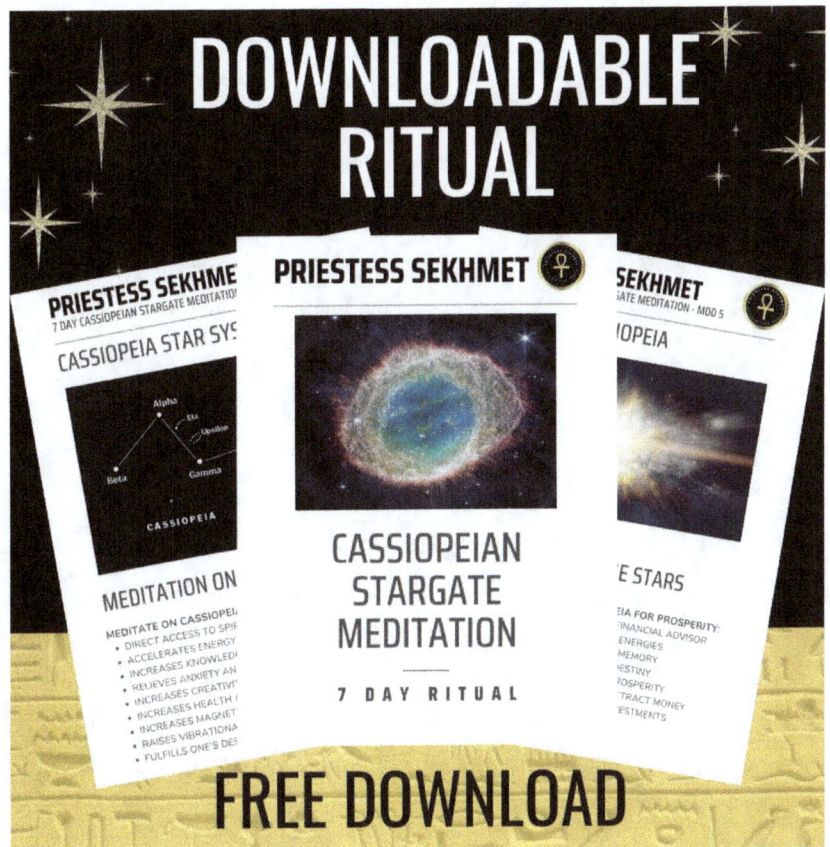

www.ingramcontent.com/pod-product-compliance
Lightning Source LLC
Chambersburg PA
CBHW062227220526
45471CB00009B/3378